Charles Dickens

Poets' Corner
in
Westminster Abbey
2nd Edition

by

Joel W. Athey, Ph.D.

Poets' Corner in Westminster Abbey
Second Edition, 2011

ISBN 978-0-615-47348-2

Published in the United States of America
DSJ Printing, Inc., Santa Monica, California

Contents

In the poetical quarter, I found there were poets who had no monuments, and monuments which had no poets... When I look upon the tombs of the great, every emotion of envy dies in me; when I read the epitaphs of the beautiful, every inordinate desire goes out; when I meet with the grief of parents upon a tombstone, my heart melts with compassion; when I see the tomb of the parents themselves, I consider the vanity of grieving for those whom we must quickly follow. When I see kings lying by those who deposed them, when I consider rival wits placed side by side, or the holy men that divided the world with their contests and disputes, I reflect with sorrow and astonishment on the little competitions, factions and debates of mankind. When I read the several dates of the tombs, of some that dy'd yesterday, and some six hundred years ago, I consider that great day when we shall all of us be contemporaries, and make our appearance together.

– Joseph Addison, *The Spectator* (March 30, 1711)

An Abbey for the Ages

An Abbey for the Ages

Poets live and die, but their works live forever. In Poets' Corner in Westminster Abbey we find the tombs of many of the greatest English poets, a term that includes dramatists and novelists as well. A walk through Poets' Corner is a tour through literary history. And we are not the first to enjoy viewing the Abbey's tombs, because the fascinating 17th-century diaries of Samuel Pepys recorded his trysts – and his dismay at missed assignations – in the Abbey, to romance among the monuments.

For over nine centuries English monarchs have been crowned – and buried – in Westminster Abbey. Edward the Confessor built a new church in the Norman style to replace the Saxon church already there, completing the work in fifteen years, just in time for his own burial in 1066 in front of the High Altar.

Building the present cathedral in the Gothic style began under Henry III in 1245 and lasted for over two hundred and fifty years.

This meant, of course, changes in Master Builders and their plans. With Henry VIII and Elizabeth I, the church switched from Catholic to Anglican interests. In the 17th century the Puritans wreaked great destruction on the altars and art. The restoration of the monarchy in 1660 overturned the Puritan influence, whereby even Oliver Cromwell was disinterred from his resting place in Westminster Abbey and hung on the gallows, his head then set on a pike for all to see.

To be buried in the Abbey came to represent the highest honor, although this conferral of status gained its greatest momentum in the 18th and 19th centuries. Before that time, a variety of people were already interred here – not only kings, queens and statesmen, but also clergymen, wives, workers at the Abbey, and an unknown child found dead in the Dark Cloister. By the early 19th century, Lord Nelson could proclaim before the sea battle at Cape St. Vincent, "Westminster Abbey, or Victory!"

During the Victorian age, the Abbey achieved its position as a truly national institution by including a wider range of religious expression within the Anglican family. In contrast, burial in the Abbey became restricted to the eminent, and the tombs became more elaborate. The most popular news was probably the installation of a heating system to replace the Abbey's warming pans.

The air raids of the Great Blitz (May 10-11, 1941) inflicted great damage on the Abbey. The spectrum of air attacks across London exhausted the water supply, which may have inadvertently saved the Abbey because the roof, all ablaze, broke away from the stone walls, fell 130 feet to the floor below and burned itself out. Post-war restorations have added color and light to the Abbey, and in the case of the North Aisle, for example, installation of superior glass in place of older glasswork.

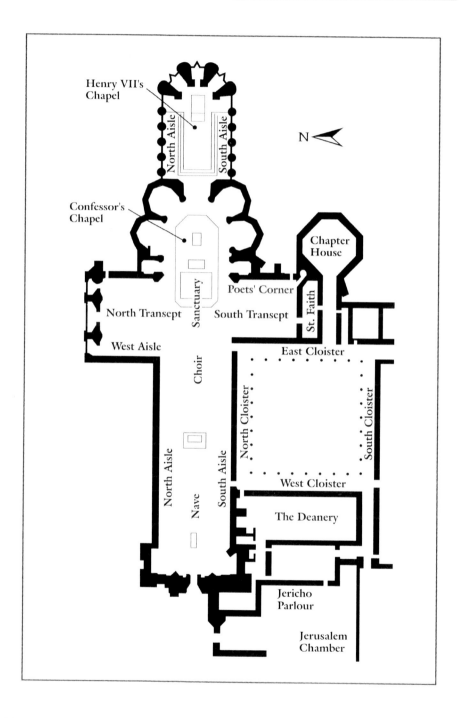

Henry VII's Chapel

North Aisle

South Aisle

N

Confessor's Chapel

Chapter House

Sanctuary

Poets' Corner

St. Faith

North Transept

South Transept

West Aisle

East Cloister

Choir

North Cloister

South Cloister

North Aisle

South Aisle

West Cloister

Nave

The Deanery

Jericho Parlour

Jerusalem Chamber

Who is Buried in Poets' Corner?

A story lies behind each of the interments in Poets' Corner. Thomas Hardy's ashes are here, but his heart was removed and buried in Dorset. Ben Jonson was buried standing upright because he could not afford a complete plot. John Gay, the mirthful author of *The Beggar's Opera*, penned his own epitaph:

> Life is a jest; and all things show it.
> I thought so once; but now I know it.

These lines met with scant approval when unveiled in 1733, and they have since been transferred to the Triforium, in the upper gallery.

Some of the greatest writers did not want to be buried here: Charles Dickens considered the privilege distastefully public; others such as Joseph Addison and William Congreve opted for interment among lords of the realm – no mere poets for them. Dramatist Richard Brinsley Sheridan sought burial among the lords but was stuck in Poets' Corner anyway.

Geoffrey Chaucer set the standard; he was the first great English poet (we don't know the name of the *Beowulf* poet). Usually linked with Shakespeare and Milton as one-third of England's poetic triumvirate, Chaucer was a high public official and tenant on the Abbey grounds when he died. Two centuries later, Edmund Spenser requested burial alongside the master poet. Thus, a tradition was born.

Chaucer

NEAR THIS STONE LIE BURIED
GEOFFREY CHAVCER 1400 JOHN DRYDEN 17
FRANCIS BEAVMONT 1616 CHARLES DE S! DENIS
SIR JOHN DENHAM 1669 LORD OF S! EVREMOND 170
SIR ROBERT MORAY MATTHEW PRIOR 172

Who is buried in Westminster Abbey? Many of its residents were once England's greatest figures, including Queen Elizabeth I, as well as Isaac Newton and Charles Darwin. Near the main west entrance, the inscription on the tomb of the Unknown Soldier reads, "They buried him among the kings." So too are the Abbey's poets, including Spenser, whose monument hangs on the south wall where chairs are often stacked, and Charles Dickens, Alfred Lord Tennyson and Robert Browning from the Victorian era. Some greats have fallen out of style, such as Victorian novelist Edward Bulwer-Lytton and poets Rudyard Kipling and John Masefield; Michael Drayton, who followed Ben Jonson as Poet Laureate, wrote the epic *Poly-Olbion* – but in the epic world, only the quintessence of a John Milton has a chance to sustain our interests, so Drayton is both gone and forgotten.

The question of *who* is buried in Poets' Corner is confused by the monuments to people who are not buried here, as well as dedications to authors whose behavior, at least on the surface, did not reflect the values of the Abbey. Shakespeare is not buried here, for example, although his statue (erected 1737) is prominent. As all the world knows, he rests in Stratford. The composer George Friederic Händel is buried here, even though he was German; he lived his last forty-seven years in England. Matthew Arnold, T. S. Eliot, and the World War I poets, among others, are not buried here. Thomas Hardy, as noted, is for the most part here, even though he was an atheist (or a theist at best).

Equally surprising are the dedications to authors whose philosophies did not coincide with the Church. The poet Percy Bysshe Shelley was expelled from Oxford for his atheistic tract. George Eliot, the great novelist and contemporary of Dickens, was also an atheist. Poet Gerard Manley Hopkins was a Jesuit. Lord Byron was as well known for his social exploits as he was for poetry. D. H. Lawrence, author of *Women In Love* and *Lady Chatterley's Lover*, was also an extremist (sex again!). In 1995 on Valentine's Day, a stained-glass window was installed high above the Matthew Arnold plaque to commemorate Oscar Wilde, whose life is reflected more in his wit than his orthodoxy: "Morality is simply the attitude we adopt to people whom we personally dislike," wrote Oscar.

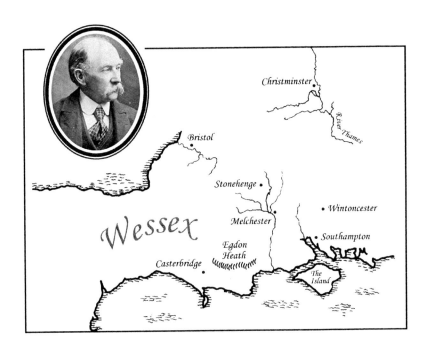

It is the greatest tribute to the Abbey that, as well as providing a final resting place for the holy, it memorializes poets based on their worthiness as people who enjoyed and shaped English life and who also contributed to the culture and pleasure of the world's people.

This is their grandest monument of all!

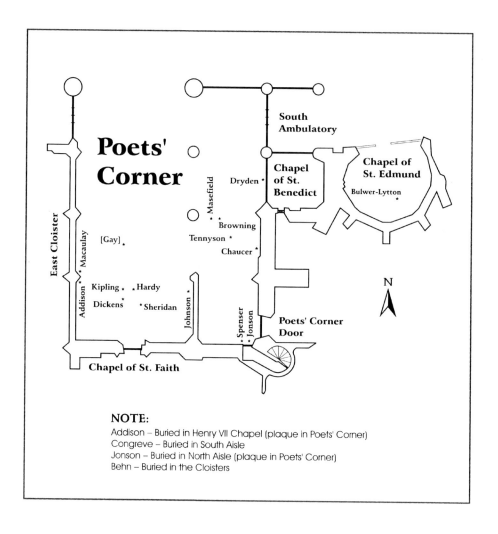

NOTE:
Addison – Buried in Henry VII Chapel (plaque in Poets' Corner)
Congreve – Buried in South Aisle
Jonson – Buried in North Aisle (plaque in Poets' Corner)
Behn – Buried in the Cloisters

Strange Bedfellows

The poets now buried in Westminster Abbey were once as varied as their genius. Although John Dryden held only a rough appreciation for Chaucer, they are now settled next to each other. In the 17th and 18th centuries the metrics used in Middle English, with its varying inflections, was a lost art, prompting Dryden to describe Chaucer's verse as having the "rude sweetness of a Scotch tune." Dryden denoted "thousands of his verses which are lame for want of half a foot, and sometimes a whole one, and which no pronunciation can make otherwise." Today we consider Chaucer's poetry metrical as well as musical – and an enormous delight.

In the Abbey we witness history's wise amalgamation. Dryden, as reported in *The Post Boy* (May 17, 1700), "was interred with Chaucer, Cowley, &c." A letter of Samuel Pepys indicated that Dryden was buried in Chaucer's grave, but surely this was an exaggeration. Part of Chaucer's gravestone was cut away to allow for the burial; however, Chaucer's remains had been moved to a new tomb long before Dryden's death. Originally buried where the Dryden bust now stands, Chaucer's remains, we think, are contained in the present tomb, erected in 1556. Dryden's bust itself has been altered, for originally the head was crowned with laurel and the statue enshrined. The bust was erected twenty years after Dryden's death, so some siting inaccuracy was already underway.

As the vocabulary and rhythms of poetry changed over time, so it is the nature of the English language to evolve. Two inventions markedly affected the pace of those changes: the first was the printing press, the second was the English dictionary. Both regularized English, not preventing changes but slowing down the inevitable process. Even as late as the 18th century, preceding Samuel Johnson's dictionary of 1755, writers expressed fears that their poetry would be lost on future generations who simply would not expend the effort to know what their ancestors were saying.

The best examples of this in the Abbey are Chaucer, whose verse comes to us in manuscript form, and Spenser, who lived in Shakespeare's time, a century after the advent of printing in England. Hence, Spenser's language is early Modern English, rather than Chaucer's Middle English (not Old English, the language of *Beowulf*, which is largely unfathomable to modern readers without help). If young students bemoan reading *Hamlet* (and certainly Spenser's *The Faerie Queene*) because of its old-fashioned language, the usage is still very recognizable English, as seen in hundreds of Shakespearean phrases we still quote, such as the heading for this section: "Misery acquaints a man with strange bedfellows" (*The Tempest*, II, ii).

Although language changes from Chaucer's time to our own were far more tumultuous, for the most part we can understand his lines without a glossary. Some specialized vocabulary is necessary (*eek* for "also"), but most meanings are readily decipherable; a passage from *The Wife of Bath's Prologue* describes her domination of her five husbands in this way:

> But sith I hadde hem hoolly in myn hond,
> And sith they hadde me yeven al hir lond,
>
> [But since I had them wholly in my hand,
> And since they had given me all their land,]

She is clear enough on which husbands she preferred: "The thre were goode men, and riche, and olde." Her use of *engendrure* for "to engender" is accessible in context of her bawdy discussion of sex.

The Abbey's procession of poets reads like a textbook on the evolution and usage of English. Witness the eloquent prose of Joseph Addison with his clarity and simplicity, of Samuel Johnson with his long, balanced arguments, and of Thomas Babington Macaulay with his rich oratorical style. Tennyson's poetry is sensuous and luxurious; Kipling's is the talk of soldiers.

Furthermore, when we study the poets' lives, we encounter their personal agendas in politics and romance as well as the frustrations that life cast in their paths. And often, we hear their wit in response. For example, Richard Brinsley Sheridan, the *bon vivant* playwright, served in Parliament for thirty-two years, yet died partly of drink and certainly in poverty. But his conversations reflected spontaneous brilliance. He ran the Drury Lane playhouse, which at one time showcased Monk Lewis' *The Castle Spectre*, a very popular Gothic drama. Sheridan, however, never gave Lewis any of the profits, which raised Lewis' ire. In Lord Byron's version:

> One day Lewis being in company with him, said, – 'Sheridan, I will make you a large bet.' Sheridan, who was always ready to make a wager, (however he might find it inconvenient to pay it if lost,) asked eagerly what bet? 'All the profits of my *Castle Spectre*,' replied Lewis. 'I will tell you what,' said Sheridan, (who never found his match at repartee,) 'I will make you a very small one, – what it is worth.'

Such stories of wit and wisdom abound for Ben Jonson, Samuel Johnson, Charles Dickens, Robert Browning, indeed for all the members of the "dead poets society" now residing silently in the Abbey. Their words, their lives, even their tombs, make for wonderful reading.

read the epitaphs of the beautiful, every inordinate
desire goes out; when I meet with the grief of
parent upon a tombstone, my heart melts with compassion; when I see the tomb of the parents themselves, I consider the vanity of grieving for those
whom we must quickly follow; when I see kings
lying by those who deposed them, or the holy men that
rival wits placed side by side, or the holy men that
divided the world with their contests and disputes, I
reflect with sorrow and astonishment on the little
competitions, factions, and debates of mankind.
When I read the several dates of the tombs, of some
that died yesterday, and some six hundred years ago,
I consider that great day when we shall all of us be
contemporaries, and make our appearance together.

[March 30, 1711.]

WESTMINSTER ABBEY. 75

mouldering earth that some time or other had a place
in the composition of a human body. Upon this I
began to consider with myself, what inn...
multitudes of people lay confus...
pavement of that...
won...

MEDITATIONS IN WESTMINSTER
ABBEY.

Pallida mors æquo pulsat pede pauperum tabernas
Regumque turres. O beate Sesti,
Vitæ summa brevis spem nos vetat inchoare longam.
Jam te premet nox, fabulæque manes,
Et domus exilis Plutonia —— —HOR.

WHEN I am in a serious humour, I very often
walk by myself in Westminster Abbey;
where the gloominess of the place, and the use to which
it is applied, with the solemnity of the building, and
the condition of the people who lie in it, are apt to fill
the mind with a kind of melancholy, that is not disagreeable. I yesterday passed a
whole afternoon in the churchyard, the cloisters, and
the church, amusing myself with the tombstones and
inscriptions that I met with in those several regions
of

of the dead. Most of them recorded nothing else of
the buried person, but that he was born upon one
day, and died upon another: the whole history of
his life being comprehended in those two circum-
stances, that are common to all mankind. I could
not but look upon these registers of existence,
whether of brass or marble, as a kind of satire upon
the departed persons; who had left no other memorial
of them, but that they were born and that they died.
They put me in mind of several persons mentioned
in the battles of heroic poems, who have sounding
names given them, for no other reason but that they
may be killed, and are celebrated for nothing but
being knocked on the head.

Γλαῦκόν τε, Μεδόντα τε, Θερσίλοχόν τε.

Glaucumque, Medontaque, Thersilochumque.

The life of these men is finely described in Holy
Writ by 'the path of an arrow,' which is immediately closed up and lost.

Upon my going into the church, I entertained myself with the digging of a grave; and saw in every
shovel-full of it that was thrown up, the fragment of
a bone or skull intermixed with a kind of fresh
mouldering

The Poets

Chaucer's Tombstone

Geoffrey Chaucer
c. 1343 - 1400

Geoffrey Chaucer was the first great English poet. His late Middle English language was inflected differently than ours, especially with the final -e pronounced, and was very musical as well as metrical. The opening lines to *The Canterbury Tales*,

Whan that Aprill with his shoures soote
The droghte of March hath perced to
   the roote,

are among the most famous in English literature.

Because Chaucer was a political man, more is known about him than Shakespeare, whose language was early Modern English. Chaucer's year of birth is unknown, but he served in a military expedition to France in 1359, where he was taken prisoner and ransomed (the King paid £16). He later traveled on diplomatic missions to Italy and probably Ireland. Chaucer married into the family of John of Gaunt, received an annuity of £10, and a pension from the King for a daily pitcher of wine. In 1369 he again served in France, then moved to Aldgate as Controller of Customs and Subsidy of Wools, Skins and Hides. Upon retiring to Kent, he was elected Knight of the Shire, but he accepted later appointments. One post he relinquished was Clerk of the King's Works, because he was robbed and beaten on several occasions. The King further granted Chaucer a butt of wine yearly. Chaucer took out a 53-year lease on a house in the garden of Westminster Abbey (where the Henry VII chapel is now located) but died nine months later.

Chaucer's first masterpiece, *Troilus and Criseyde*, is a sustained narration of heroism with some comic insights. The poem employs the conventions of courtly love and knighthood, as well as contributes "pander" (from Pandarus) to our language. In *The Canterbury Tales*, the 30 pilgrims agree to tell four tales each, although only 24 get told. The entourage includes the worthy Knight, the effeminate Pardoner ("I trowe he were a geldyng or a mare"), the drunken Miller whose tale of a naive carpenter losing his wife's favors to a shrewd miller is rebutted by a vengeful Reeve who is a carpenter, and others. The assertive Wife of Bath, having outlived five husbands, declares, "welcome the sixte, whan that evere he shal." Her own desires are clear ("I nyl envye no virginitee"), as well as her justification of sex,

Thanne were they maad upon a creature
To purge uryne, and eek for engendrure.

Chaucer was buried in the Abbey partly because he was a resident of the grounds, partly because he was a notable courtier, certainly because he was a great poet. His sarcophagus was installed in 1556, although his remains were originally buried somewhere near the present Dryden statue slightly to the north. Its inscription reads, "to the glory of my mother-country's poetry."

The Pardoner

from The Wife of Bath's Prologue

Now, sire, now wol I telle forth my tale. –
As evere moote I drynken wyn or ale,
I shal seye sooth, tho housbondes that I hadde,
As thre of hem were goode, and two were badde.
The thre were goode men, and riche, and olde;
Unnethe myghte they the statut holde
In which that they were bounden unto me.
Ye woot wel what I meene of this, pardee!
As help me God, I laughe whan I thynke
How pitously a-nyght I made hem swynke!
And, by my fey, I tolde of it no stoor.
They had me yeven hir lond and hir tresoor;
Me neded nat do lenger diligence
To wynne hir love, or doon hem reverence.
They loved me so wel, by God above,
That I ne tolde no deyntee of hir love!
A wys womman wol bisye hire evere in oon
To gete hire love, ye, ther as she hath noon.
But sith I hadde hem hoolly in myn hond,
And sith they hadde me yeven al hir lond,
What sholde I taken keep hem for to plese,
But it were for my profit and myn ese?
I sette hem so a-werke, by my fey,
That many a nyght they songen 'weilawey!'
The bacon was not fet for hem, I trowe,
That som men han in Essex at Dunmowe.
I governed hem so wel, after my lawe,
That ech of hem ful blisful was and fawe
To brynge me gaye thynges fro the fayre.
They were ful glad whan I spak to hem faire;
For, God it woot, I chidde hem spitously.

Edmund Spenser
c. 1552 - 1599

Edmund Spenser was the poets' poet, employing exquisite verse forms and rich language rivalled later only by John Keats and Alfred Tennyson. *The Faerie Queene*, a long allegory celebrating Protestantism, England and Queen Elizabeth, was his masterpiece.

Little is known of Spenser's early life; only two lines in *Prothalamion* testify that he was born in London:

To mery London, my most kyndly nurse,
That to me gave this lifes first native sourse.

He received a B.A. and M.A. from Cambridge and counted among his friends Sir Philip Sidney, the Earl of Leicester (once, the Queen's favorite) and Sir Walter Raleigh (a later favorite). In 1580, as secretary to Lord Grey, the new Lord Deputy, Spenser moved to Ireland, which became home for the rest of his life. He witnessed first-hand the military actions and devastation resulting from brutal Anglo-Irish conflicts. As a man of political affairs, he acquired a large estate, and at the time of his death was nominated for sheriff of Cork. The Irish uprising of 1598 and the burning of his home probably hastened his death

The Faerie Queene features Una and the Red Cross Knight, Sir Guyon, the Knight of Temperance, Artegall, and Britomart in their struggles against evil and slander. The poem's medievalism is enhanced by Spenser's lavish, deliberately contrived antique language, epic similes and the new Spenserian stanza (9 lines, ending in a slow Alexandrine). Its morality is evident in his dedication, "to fashion a gentleman or noble person in vertuous and gentle discipline." The poem remains unfinished.

The legend that Spenser died in poverty is probably untrue, although his estate had been ransacked and his family fled to Cork awaiting English troops. Spenser carried the siege letter to London, where he died three weeks after his arrival. Spenser was buried near Chaucer, with verse elegies thrown into his grave. The monument erected 20 years later erred in the birth date (by 40 years) and the death date (by 3 years); the misspelling of his name was acceptable in an age before spelling was regularized. The present marble slab on the south wall replaced the earlier one in 1778 and corrected the dates. In 1938 permission was granted to open the tomb in hopes of finding a poem by Shakespeare, but public protest prevented this. Also, there is no certainty where the coffin is. No reliable portrait or other likeness exists for Spenser.

> One day I wrote her name upon the strand,
> But came the waves and washed it away:
> Agayne I wrote it with a second hand,
> But came the tyde, and made my paynes his pray.
> 'Vayne man,' sayd she, 'that doest in vaine assay,
> A mortall thing so to immortalize,'
> *from Sonnet 75*

from The Faerie Queene *(Bk. 1, Canto 11)*

With that they heard a roaring hideous sound,
  That all the ayre with terrour filled wide,
  And seem'd uneath to shake the stedfast ground.
  Eftsoones that dreadfull Dragon they espide,
  Where stretcht he lay upon the sunny side
  Of a great hill, himselfe like a great hill.
  But all so soone, as he from far descride
  Those glistring armes, that heaven with light did fill,
He rousd himselfe full blith, and hastned them untill.

                    . . .

And that more wondrous was, in either jaw
  Threeranckes of yron teeth enraunged were,
  In which yet trickling bloud and gobbets raw
  Of late devoured bodies did appeare,
  That sight thereof bred cold congealed feare:
  Which to increase, and all at once to kill,
  A cloud of smoothering smoke and sulphur seare
  Out of his stinking gorge forth steemed still,
That all the ayre about with smoke and stench did fill.

The knight gan fairely couch his steadie speare,
  And fiercely ran at him with rigorous might:
  The pointed steele arriving rudely theare,
  His harder hide would neither perce, nor bight,
  But glauncing by forth passed forward right;
  Yet sore amoved with so puissant push,
  The wrathfull beast about him turned light,
  And him so rudely passing by, did brush
With his long tayle, that horse and man to ground did rush.

Ben Jonson
1572 - 1637

Soldier, duelist, actor, playwright and poet, Ben Jonson is remembered chiefly as a satirist; his plays *Volpone* (1606) and *The Alchemist* (1610) adapt supremely well to modernizations. In 1616 Jonson became England's first Poet Laureate, and unofficially the head of a "school" of poets, the Sons of Ben.

Rough and rambunctious, Jonson killed his enemy in hand-to-hand combat during the war against Spain. Later, as an actor, he skewered a fellow-actor in a duel and escaped justice by pleading "benefit of clergy" (because he could read Latin). He battled fellow playwrights on the boards, yet was a dear friend of Shakespeare, encapsulating the universal judgment of the Bard in his Preface to the First Folio: "He was not of an age, but for all time!" Shakespeare had acted in Jonson's first success, *Every Man in His Humour*. In his audacity, Jonson published his own collected works in 1616, a first in England.

Both *Volpone* and *The Alchemist* ridicule greed and guile, bitter comic romps where rascals pray on equally loathsome society scamps whose only concerns are commercial. Jonson's poetry ranges from wit to controlled melancholy, demonstrating his mastery of versification. "To Celia" is his oft-quoted love poem for the ages.

Jonson lies buried in the North Aisle of the Nave. Vertically! He was too poor to merit a spot alongside Chaucer and Spenser in Poets' Corner. In his own words to the Dean of Westminster, "too poor for that, and no one will lay out funeral charges upon me. No, sir, six feet long by two feet wide is too much for me; two feet by two feet will do." And so it did!

Come, my Celia, let us prove,
While we can, the sports of love;
Time will not be ours forever,
He, at length, our good will sever;
Spend not then his gifts in vain.
Suns that set may rise again;
But if once we lose this light,
'Tis with us perpetual night.
Why should we defer our joys?
–from Volpone

His epitaph was paid for by a passer-by, and the stonemason carved O RARE BEN JOHNSON. Whether this was intended as ORARE (Latin for "Pray for") and only the vague spacing renders it an English meaning, no one knows. (Note the *h* in the name.) The epitaph is prominently displayed on his monument on the south wall of Poets' Corner, again on the floor where he "stands," and on the original as it was transferred to the floorboard immediately north of his resting spot in the North Aisle.

Indeed, he was rare.

Song: To Celia

Drink to me only with thine eyes,
    And I will pledge with mine;
Or leave a kiss but in the cup,
    And I'll not look for wine.
The thirst, that from the soul doth rise,
    Doth ask a drink divine:
But might I of Jove's nectar sup,
    I would not change for thine.

I sent thee late a rosy wreath,
    Not so much honouring thee,
As giving it a hope, that there
    It could not wither'd be.
But thou thereon didst only breathe,
    And sent'st it back to me;
Since when it grows and smells, I swear,
    Not of itself, but thee.

John Dryden
1631 - 1700

John Dryden was the leading poet, dramatist and critic of the Restoration period. His precise, lucid style, which mirrored the scientific spirit of the Royal Society, made him the least personal of the great English poets. He was appointed Poet Laureate in 1668 but lost his office twenty years later.

Dryden earned his B.A. from Cambridge and wrote poetry, but his first success came as a playwright. His plays were very formal, with Herculean heroes in epic conflicts told in rhymed couplets. *All for Love*, a retelling of Shakespeare's *Antony and Cleopatra*, was less grandiose but more popular. He also wrote successful comedies. Dryden, who published the first comprehensive literary criticism, is called the "father of English criticism." His greatest poems were verse satires. One Dryden controversy involved his perceived opportunism: He praised Cromwell, then became a Protestant supporter of Charles II, who granted him the Laureateship. When James II, a Catholic, succeeded to the throne, Dryden converted. However, when James was forced out, Dryden stuck by his Catholicism, losing his offices and stipends. He supported himself by translating Virgil, Chaucer and others, although he died poor.

The plain style sharpened his arguments and avoided the affectations of the baroque style of preceding eras. This was ideal for the thrust and parry of quick logic useful in satire. The poetic mode was the heroic couplet, a pair of rhymed lines that contains a complete idea. Perfected by Dryden, this form remained the poetic vehicle for Pope and Johnson in the next century. The poem may be long – his great satire *Absalom and Achitophel* is 1030 lines – but the whole is comprised of rhyming couplets. The subject matter was serious, distancing the Catholic crisis of succession in terms of the biblical King David. *Mac Flecknoe* is an outrageous mock epic portraying Thomas Shadwell, who became Poet Laureate when Dryden was ousted, as the ideal inheritor of the throne of dullness. The epic stance seemed solemn, but the description of Shadwell was hilarious:

Success let others teach, learn thou
from me
Pangs without birth, and fruitless
industry.

Dryden was buried twice, first at St. Anne's in Soho, but a few days later exhumed, embalmed and buried with full ceremony next to the Chaucer sarcophagus.

from Mac Flecknoe

All human things are subject to decay,
And when fate summons, monarchs must obey.
This Flecknoe found, who, like Augustus, young
Was called to empire, and had governed long;
In prose and verse, was owned, without dispute,
Through all the realms of Nonsense, absolute.
This aged prince, now flourishing in peace,
And blest with issue of a large increase,
Worn out with business, did at length debate
To settle the succession of the state;
And, pondering which of all his sons was fit
To reign, and wage immortal war with wit,
Cried: ' 'Tis resolved; for nature pleads that he
Should only rule, who most resembles me.
Sh____ alone my perfect image bears,
Mature in dullness from his tender years:
Sh____ alone, of all my sons, is he
Who stands confirmed in full stupidity.
The rest to some faint meaning make pretense,
But Sh____ never deviates into sense.
Some beams of wit on other souls may fall,
Strike through, and make a lucid interval;
But Sh____'s genuine night admits no ray,
His rising fogs prevail upon the day.
Besides, his goodly fabric fills the eye,
And seems designed for thoughtless majesty:
Thoughtless as monarch oaks that shade the plain,
And, spread in solemn state, supinely reign.
Heywood and Shirley were but types of thee,
Thou last great prophet of tautology.

William Congreve
1670 - 1729

William Congreve was the greatest comic playwright of his era and one of the greatest in all of English theater. His *The Way of the World* (1700) was the epitome of the sparkling, usually licentious dramas of the Restoration period. He wrote only five plays, four of which were comedies, then at age 30 retired to life as a gentleman.

Born in England but raised in Cork County, Ireland, Congreve took up residence in London at age 20. His many friends, including Dryden, Pope, Swift and Addison, served as testimony to his congeniality and wit. However, he was plagued by gout and cataracts, and ill health became a constant problem. In later years he was companion to the Duchess of Marlborough, the wealthiest woman in England.

Restoration comedies of manners were romantic intrigues about wives, husbands and other lovers; their satire aimed at fops and coquettes of fashionable society. Congreve became master of such intellectualized licentiousness and witty dialogue. His titles suggest this spirit: *The Old Bachelor*, *The Double Dealer*, *Love for Love*, and *The Way of the World*. Character names tell us even more: Witwoud, Petulant, Fainall, and Lady Wishfort.

Mirabell and Millimant are his spirited lovers in *The Way of the World*. This, his greatest play, was not an overwhelming success because the vogue shifted to sentimental comedies where rakes were not really so wicked and ladies kept their virtue intact. In *The Mourning Bride*, Congreve wrote, "music has charms to soothe a savage breast" and "nor hell a fury, like a woman scorn'd" (which we often say, "hell hath no fury like a woman scorned").

Congreve was emphatic that he was not a writer, rather a gentleman who wrote. Consequently, when he died from a coach accident, he was buried in the South Aisle close to the front entrance; the Prime Minister was one of his pall-bearers. The Duchess of Marlborough erected his monument, but got the dates wrong: perhaps she desired a "younger man," for this epitaph dropped two years (he was 58). Her own mother mocked the inscription, "I know not what *pleasure* she might have had in his company, but I am sure it was no *honor*." The grieving Duchess ordered a dressed, ivory figure of Congreve to sit at her dinner table so she could talk to it, and her servants changed the bandages on its "gouty" feet.

from The Way of the World *(Act II)*

MIRABELL: You seem to be unattended, madam. You used to have the *beau monde* throng after you; and a flock of gay fine perukes hovering round you.

WITWOUD: Like moths about a candle. I had like to have lost my comparison for want of breath.

MILLAMANT: Oh, I have denied myself airs today. I have walked as fast through the crowd –

WITWOUD: As a favorite in disgrace, and with as few followers.

MILLAMANT: Dear Mr. Witwoud, truce with your similitudes: for I am as sick of 'em –

WITWOUD: As a physician of a good air. I cannot help it, madam, though 'tis against myself.

MILLAMANT: Yet again! Mincing, stand between me and his wit.

WITWOUD: Do, Mrs. Mincing, like a screen before a great fire. I confess I do blaze today; I am too bright.

MRS. FAINALL: But, dear Millamant, why were you so long?

MILLAMANT: Long! Lord, have I not made violent haste? I have asked every living thing I met for you; I have inquired after you, as after a new fashion.

WITWOUD: Madam, truce with your similitudes. No, you met her husband, and did not ask him for her.

MIRABELL: By your leave, Witwoud, that were like inquiring after an old fashion, to ask a husband for his wife.

WITWOUD: Hum, a hit! a hit! a palpable hit! I confess it.

MRS. FAINALL: You were dressed before I came abroad.

MILLAMANT: Aye, that's true. Oh, but then I had – Mincing, what had I? Why was I so long?

MINCING: O mem, your la'ship stayed to peruse a pecquet of letters.

MILLAMANT: Oh, aye, letters; I had letters. I am persecuted with letters. I hate letters. Nobody knows how to write letters; and yet one has 'em, one does not know why. They serve one to pin up one's hair.

WITWOUD: Is that the way? Pray, madam, do you pin up your hair with all your letters? I find I must keep copies.

MILLAMANT: Only with those in verse, Mr. Witwoud. I never pin up my hair with prose. I fancy one's hair would not curl if it were pinned up with prose. I think I tried it once, Mincing.

MINCING: O mem, I shall never forget it.

Joseph Addison
1672 - 1719

Joseph Addison was a Latin scholar and statesman as well as a major literary figure. With his collaborator Richard Steele, he wrote and published *The Tatler* (1709-11) and *The Spectator* (1711-12). These early newspapers were folio broadsides (one sheet folded), each usually consisting of a single essay with subjects ranging from dueling or fashion to opera, Milton's poetry or the philosophy of the sublime. Often, eccentric but lovable characters voiced social views; other issues invited letters from readers, which was an early forum for reader participation.

For a growing urbane readership, Mr. Spectator declared: "I shall be ambitious to have it said of me that I brought philosophy out of closets and libraries, schools and colleges, to dwell in clubs and assemblies, at tea tables and in coffeehouses." These essays were distinguished by genial warmth and clear prose that became the hallmark of wit and reason, still today considered the *middle style* of good writing. They were enormously popular among both men and women readers.

Addison is even more impressive when his political career and personality are considered. As a Whig, he rose to become Secretary of State, in spite of a staid temperament that was scholarly and formal and a reticence that prevented him from addressing Parliament. The contrast to his collaborator was also remarkable because Steele was the carefree man-about-town, often in debt. Addison married late in life to the Dowager Countess of Warwick. On his deathbed, Addison summoned her son, the young Earl of Warwick, to declare, "See in what peace a Christian can die."

Today, Addison is seldom read and his topics are outmoded. We need a history book to remind us that the early 18th century was the Age of Addison. Addison's monument is on the west wall of Poets' Corner by Händel, but he chose to be buried with the aristocrats near his friend Lord Montague, statesman and founder of the Bank of England, not far from the tombs of Elizabeth I and Mary I in the North Aisle of Henry VII's Chapel. Oddly, no stone was placed over his burial spot until ninety years passed.

from The Spectator (No. 105)

For these reasons Will shines in mixt company, where he has the discretion not to go out of his depth, and has often a certain way of making his real ignorance appear a seeming one. Our club however has frequently caught him tripping, at which times they never spare him. For as Will often insults us with the knowledge of the town, we sometimes take our revenge upon him by our knowledge of books.

He was last week producing two or three letters which he writ in his youth to a coquet lady. The raillery of them was natural, and well enough for a mere man of the town; but, very unluckily, several of the words were wrong spelt. Will laught this off at first as well as he could, but finding himself pushed on all sides, and especially by the Templar, he told us, with a little passion, that he never liked pedantry in spelling, and that he spelt like a gentleman, and not like a scholar: upon this Will had recourse to his old topic of showing the narrow spiritedness, the pride, and ignorance of pedants; which he carried so far, that upon my retiring to my lodgings, I could not forbear throwing together such reflections as occurred to me upon that subject.

A man who has been brought up among books, and is able to talk of nothing else, is a very indifferent companion, and what we call a pedant. But, methinks, we should enlarge the title, and give it every one that does not know how to think out of his profession, and particular way of life.

What is a greater pedant than a mere man of the town? Bar him the playhouses, a catalogue of the reigning beauties, and an account of a few fashionable distempers that have befallen him, and you strike him dumb. How many a pretty gentleman's knowledge lies all within the verge of the court? He will tell you the names of the principal favourites, repeat the shrewd sayings of a man of quality, whisper an intrigue that is not yet blown upon by common fame; or, if the sphere of his observations is a little larger than ordinary, will perhaps enter into all the incidents, turns, and revolutions in a game of ombre. When he has gone thus far he has shown you the whole circle of his accomplishments, his parts are drained, and he is disabled from any farther conversation. What are these but rank pedants? and yet these are the men who value themselves most on their exemption from the pedantry of colleges.

Samuel Johnson
1709 - 1784

Doctor Johnson, the great lexicographer, was a poet and critic whose most interesting works today are his *Preface* to Shakespeare and *Lives of the Poets*. Equally important, though, was his voluminous, witty conversation recorded by James Boswell in *The Life of Samuel Johnson*. The mid-18th century is known as the Age of Johnson.

Overcoming poverty and despair, Johnson acquired enormous erudition and a strong dose of cynicism: When challenged why a man drinks to excess, Johnson replied, "He who makes a beast of himself gets rid of the pain of being a man." Johnson dropped out of Oxford, married a widow twenty years older, and moved to London. He compiled the *Dictionary* single-handedly (with six copyists) from 1747 to 1755. His dictionary defines "dull" as "not exciting, not delightful; as, to make dictionaries is *dull* work." Until 1760 he wrote for money to keep his projects afloat: two periodicals, *The Rambler* and *The Idler*; his poem *The Vanity of Human Wishes*; a play *Irene*; and *Rasselas*, a philosophical novella. ("No man but a blockhead ever wrote, except for money.") Boswell met Johnson in 1763, and his *Life* changed the nature of biographies forever, as he recorded the great volume of Johnson's words and thereby let the reader gauge the spirit of the man.

The *Dictionary* defined over 40,000 words, supported by quotes (114,000 of them) from Johnson's reading. This technique, as well as his inclusion of common words, revolutionized lexicography. Although we often remember only its witty sallies (*oats*: "a grain, which in England is generally given to horses, but in Scotland supports the people." Or, *network*: "Anything reticulated or decussated, at equal distances, with interstices between the intersections"), the great majority of definitions were extremely useful. Most important, the dictionary set standards for correct usage, slowing language change from one era to another. His *Preface* is still perhaps the best insight into Shakespeare. In *Lives of the Poets*, Johnson critiqued his subjects, using the balanced prose style of the mid-century, where each point is counterpointed. In "Milton," his sensible praise of *Paradise Lost* ends with, "no one ever wished it longer."

Johnson's position in Poets' Corner was assured, a judgment comforting to the great Tory himself. He was interred at the foot of the Shakespeare monument, with Edmund Burke, Joshua Reynolds and others serving as pallbearers. His bust was affixed in 1939 to the interior wall above his grave.

from Lives of the Poets - Pope

Of genius, that power which constitutes a poet; that quality without which judgment is cold and knowledge is inert; that energy which collects, combines, amplifies and animates; the superiority must, with some hesitation, be allowed to Dryden. It is not to be inferred that of this poetical vigor Pope had only a little, because Dryden had more; for every other writer since Milton must give place to Pope; and even of Dryden it must be said that if he has brighter paragraphs, he has not better poems. Dryden's performances were always hasty, either excited by some external occasion, or extorted by domestic necessity; he composed without consideration, and published without correction. What his mind could supply at call, or gather in one excursion, was all that he sought, and all that he gave. The dilatory caution of Pope enabled him to condense his sentiments, to multiply his images, and to accumulate all that study might produce, or chance might supply. If the flights of Dryden therefore are higher, Pope continues longer on the wing. If of Dryden's fire the blaze is brighter, of Pope's the heat is more regular and constant. Dryden often surpasses expectation, and Pope never falls below it. Dryden is read with frequent astonishment, and Pope with perpetual delight.

Richard Brinsley Sheridan
1751 - 1816

Once a duelist and later a member of Parliament, Richard Brinsley Sheridan wrote *The School for Scandal*, perhaps the sprightliest English comedy and the ultimate licentious Restoration drama. To the surprise of many moderns, this play arrived three-quarters of a century after the close of the Restoration period.

Sheridan was greatly influenced by his Dublin heritage: his parents were both theater people, and his grandfather was a friend of Jonathan Swift. The family moved to London, where young Richard attended Harrow. In love with a beautiful singer, Elizabeth Linley, Sheridan twice duelled Captain Mathews over her honor, winning the first duel but losing and getting repeatedly stabbed in the second. He married Elizabeth, managed the theater at Drury Lane, wrote *The Rivals* and *The School for Scandal* in a two-year period, and soon after retired from the theater. In 1780 Sheridan began 32 years in Parliament as an ally of Lord Fox and the Whigs. However, the fiscal havoc that defined his Drury Lane days, along with alcohol and other extravagances, caused his political and personal demise. Creditors hounded him after the Drury Lane fire of 1809, and eventually he spent time in jail for debts and died in poverty.

His great comedies of manners lampoon the pomposity of social prigs and careless lovers. Their success resides mainly in witty dialogue. *The Rivals* will live forever because of Mrs. Malaprop, who says "reprehend" for "comprehend," "perpetrated" for "perfected," "He is the very pineapple of politeness," and "She's as headstrong as an allegory on the banks of the Nile." Plot strands are both comic and sentimental. In *The School for Scandal*, Lady Sneerwell, Snake, Joseph Surface and Sir Peter Teazle dramatize social disharmony. Sheridan's comic touch is showcased in the auction scene where the hero maintains a sensitive vulnerability and in the screen scene where the hypocrites are exposed in crass embarrassment.

Sheridan wanted to be buried alongside Lord Fox, but apparently politics prevented this. Instead, he was interred in Poets' Corner next to the great actor David Garrick. His pallbearers and funeral attendees were lords and earls. Lord Byron wrote that Sheridan could be compared to Fox and Edmund Burke as a man of principle, and "with none in talent, for he beat them all out and out."

> *If I reprehend anything in this world, it is the use of my oracular tongue, and a nice derangement of epitaphs!*
> –Mrs. Malaprop, The Rivals

from The School for Scandal *(Act IV)*

LADY TEAZLE: Well, well, I'm inclined to believe you. But isn't it provoking, to have the most ill-natured things said to one? And there's my friend Lady Sneerwell has circulated I don't know how many scandalous tales of me! and all without any foundation, too – that's what vexes me.

JOSEPH SURFACE: Aye, madam, to be sure, that is the provoking circumstance – without foundation! yes, yes, there's the mortification, indeed; for, when a scandalous story is believed against one, there certainly is no comfort like the consciousness of having deserved it.

LADY TEAZLE: No, to be sure – then I'd forgive their malice; but to attack me, who am really so innocent, and who never say an ill-natured thing of anybody – that is, of any friend – and then Sir Peter, too, to have him so peevish, and so suspicious, when I know the integrity of my own heart – indeed 'tis monstrous!

JOSEPH SURFACE: But, my dear Lady Teazle, 'tis your own fault if you suffer it. When a husband entertains a groundless suspicion of his wife, and withdraws his confidence from her, the original compact is broke, and she owes it to the honor of her sex to endeavor to outwit him.

Thomas Babington Macaulay

1800 - 1859

Lord Macaulay wrote popular essays and histories that reflected the Whig philosophy of material progress and English commerce. These secured his entrance into Parliament. Macaulay became the nineteenth century's most eminent man of letters.

As the son of a former governor of Sierra Leone whose evangelical fervor helped abolish the slave trade (1807) and slavery itself in the British dominions (1833), Macaulay saw that a nation's need is determined by the moral and cultural climate of its times. He studied law at Cambridge, entered Parliament in 1830, served four years in India on the Supreme Council, then returned to England and a seat in Parliament. His speech on the Ten-Hours Bill (limiting child labor) was brilliant. His memory was so astonishing that he once stated that if every copy of *Paradise Lost* and *Pilgrim's Progress* were lost, he could reproduce them from recall. Macaulay wrote essays, then produced his *History of England* and a verse narrative, *Lays of Ancient Rome*. Today Macaulay's works go largely unread, but in his time they were eagerly anticipated, and he became the first man elevated to the peerage due to his literary efforts.

> *The Puritan hated bear-baiting, not because it gave pain to the bear, but because it gave pleasure to the spectators.*
>
> –*History of England*

Macaulay's histories supported the Whig optimism that English life was made better by commerce, invention and the accumulation of wealth. His essay on Francis Bacon advocated a pragmatic philosophy: "An acre in Middlesex is better than a principality in Utopia." Influenced by Walter Scott's novels, Macaulay "invented" writing history that included the commonplace realities of daily life, to portray an entire society at its point in history. Like Scott, he sometimes invented scenes, but all in the name of readable history. Consequently, his four-volume *History of England* from 1685 to the Reform Bill of 1832 advanced only to the year 1702. His essay on Lord Clive, conqueror of India, was as much descriptive narration as argument. Macaulay's prose, like his oratory, was clear, rich, sonorous and, above all, interesting.

Both Macaulay and his father lie in Westminster Abbey: Zachary Macaulay's bust in the north nave, just inside the front entrance; the son buried in Poets' Corner under Addison's statue.

from Lord Clive

Clive was in a painfully anxious situation. He could place no confidence in the sincerity or in the courage of his confederate; and, whatever confidence he might place in his own military talents, and in the valour and discipline of his troops, it was no light thing to engage an army twenty times as numerous as his own. Before him lay a river over which it was easy to advance, but over which, if things went ill, not one of his little band would ever return. On this occasion, for the first and for the last time, his dauntless spirit, during a few hours, shrank from the fearful responsibility of making a decision. He called a council of war. The majority pronounced against fighting; and Clive declared his concurrence with the majority. Long afterwards, he said that he had never called but one council of war, and that, if he had taken the advice of that council, the British would never have been

masters of Bengal. But scarcely had the meeting broken up when he was himself again. He retired alone under the shade of some trees, and passed near an hour there in thought. He came back determined to put everything to the hazard, and gave orders that all should be in readiness for passing the river on the morrow.

The battle commenced with a cannonade in which the artillery of the Nabob did scarcely any execution, while the few fieldpieces of the English produced great effect. Several of the most distinguished officers in Surajah Dowlah's service fell. Disorder began to spread through his ranks. His own terror increased every moment. One of the conspirators urged on him the expediency of retreating. The insidious advice, agreeing as it did with what his own terrors suggested, was readily received. He ordered his army to fall back, and this order decided his fate. Clive snatched the moment, and ordered his troops to advance. The confused and dispirited multitude gave way before the onset of disciplined valour. No mob attacked by regular soldiers was ever more completely routed. The little band of Frenchmen, who alone ventured to confront the English, were swept down the stream of fugitives. In an hour the forces of Surajah Dowlah were dispersed, never to reassemble. Only five hundred of the vanquished were slain. But their camp, their guns, their baggage, innumerable waggons, innumerable cattle, remained in the power of the conquerors. With the loss of twenty-two soldiers killed and fifty wounded, Clive had scattered an army of near sixty thousand men, and subdued an empire larger and more populous than Great Britain.

Charles Dickens
1812-1870

Charles Dickens was the most popular novelist in England and probably all the world. His novels are marked by bold prose, memorable characters, and social reform to benefit the poor.

Dickens' life reads like one of his novels. When his father went to debtors' prison, 12-year-old Charles perceived his world at an end, laboring at the blacking-paste factory, school over forever. At 19 his sweetheart was forbidden to marry him when her father declared that young Dickens would never amount to anything. From court reporter to novelist at age 24, to world fame just two years later, Dickens' career never faltered. He acquired renown as reader/actor of his own novels. Dickens was hailed wherever he went; even theater performances were interrupted by actors and audience alike giving "Three cheers for Charles Dickens, esquire." After ten children, he ultimately split from his wife to be with Ellen Ternan the actress. His enormous energy often resulted in writing two novels at once, plus publishing *Household Words*, campaigning for education and workers' rights, speaking on tour – yet, many letters record that he walked the streets of London all night to pass the time. He died exhausted at age 58.

The novels streamed forth: *Oliver Twist*, where the orphan audaciously begged for more porridge; *The Old Curiosity Shop*, where Little Nell's death scene was protracted for weeks; *A Christmas Carol*, where even Scrooge is moved by Tiny Tim's "God bless Us, Every One!"; *David Copperfield*, where the hero was unmistakably young Dickens himself; *Hard Times*, where Mr. Gradgrind insisted on "Facts, sir; nothing but Facts!"; *Bleak House*, where the fog was "everywhere. Fog up the river ... fog down the river"; *A Tale of Two Cities*, where Sydney Carton volunteered himself on the guillotine for the doomed Charles Darnay, "a far, far better thing that I do, than I have ever done"; *Great Expectations*, where Pip's expectations depended on Miss Havisham as well as Magwitch the convict. For over 150 years Dickens' readers have loved "the best of times ... the worst of times" (*A Tale of Two Cities*).

In his will Dickens specified an "inexpensive, unostentatious and strictly private manner" and forbade black bows, cloaks and "other such revolting absurdity" for his funeral. Rochester, his childhood home, was his selected destination, but the interests of the nation required interment in Poets' Corner, so a compromise was reached for a private ceremony there. His grave lay open for two days, and at the end of each day over 1000 people still waited outside to pay their respects.

from Oliver Twist

The evening arrived; the boys took their places. The master, in his cook's uniform, stationed himself at the copper; his pauper assistants ranged themselves behind him; the gruel was served out; and a long grace was said over the short commons. The gruel disappeared; the boys whispered each other, and winked at Oliver, while his next neighbours nudged him. Child as he was, he was desperate with hunger, and reckless with misery. He rose from the table; and advancing to the master, basin and spoon in hand, said: somewhat alarmed at his own temerity:

'Please, sir, I want some more.'

The master was a fat, healthy man; but he turned very pale. He gazed in stupefied astonishment on the small rebel for some seconds, and then clung for support to the copper. The assistants were paralysed with wonder; the boys with fear.

'What!' said the master at length, in a faint voice.

'Please, sir,' replied Oliver, 'I want some more.'

The master aimed a blow at Oliver's head with the ladle; pinioned him in his arms; and shrieked aloud for the beadle.

The board were sitting in solemn conclave, when Mr. Bumble rushed into the room in great excitement, and addressing the gentleman in the high chair, said, 'Mr. Limbkins, I beg your pardon, sir! Oliver Twist has asked for more!'

There was a general start. Horror was depicted on every countenance.

'For *more!*' said Mr. Limbkins. 'Compose yourself, Bumble, and answer me distinctly. Do I understand that he asked for more, after he had eaten the supper allotted by the dietary?'

'He did, sir,' replied Bumble.

'That boy will be hung,' said the gentleman in the white waistcoat; 'I know that boy will be hung.'

Alfred Lord Tennyson
1809 - 1892

Today it is difficult to regard a poet as central to society, but such was the position of Alfred Tennyson in Victorian England. He served as Poet Laureate from 1850 to 1892 and was knighted in 1883.

The madness that ran in Tennyson's family worried the brooding, introspective poet all his life. At Cambridge he was elected into The Apostles, an elite student body important at a time when university education was haphazard and largely left up to the undergraduates themselves. There he met Arthur Hallam – poetic like Tennyson, but stylish and aristocratic as Tennyson was not. Hallam's early death plunged Tennyson into a despair that did not abate until *In Memoriam* was published 17 years later. That year, 1850, marked the watershed of Tennyson's life, for he also married his long-betrothed Emily and succeeded William Wordsworth as Poet Laureate. From 1842, when he published his second important volume of verse, until his death, Tennyson was a major voice in English life and Victorian optimism, which included responses to religious doubt and the disaster at Balaclava in the Crimean War ("The Charge of the Light Brigade"). For over a century, publishers have respected Tennyson's wish that collections of his poetry end with "Crossing the Bar," his beautiful elegy written at age 80.

Tennyson was the poet of metrical versatility and luxurious language, a melancholic successor to the Romantic tradition. His poems embody twilight and reflection rather than daylight and activity. Stately "Ulysses" postures the aged adventurer calling for one final mission, "To strive, to seek, to find, and not to yield." Its companion, "The Lotos-Eaters," recasts the mariners' choice between duty and the opium blossom. His ballad "The Lady of Shalott" inspired John Waterhouse's painting now in the Tate Gallery:

> Down she came and found a boat
> Beneath a willow left afloat,
> And round about the prow she wrote
> *The Lady of Shalott.*

Tennyson's masterpieces, *In Memoriam* and *Idylls of the King*, were each dedicated to its respective Arthur. Tennyson's reputation sank very low after his death because critics perceived a facile moralizing. The poet who gave us "In the spring a young man's fancy lightly turns to thoughts of love" and

> 'Tis better to have loved and lost
> Than never to have loved at all.

seemed too glib. Today his reputation is secure.

Tennyson was buried in Poet's Corner near Browning and Dryden. Queen Victoria, who had corresponded with the poet for thirty years, received condolences from around the world. For the ceremony, the Abbey's nave was lined by soldiers of the Balaclava Light Brigade. His bust reposes on the corner of the intermediate wall closest to the Byron stone.

The Charge of the Light Brigade

Half a league, half a league,
Half a league onward,
All in the valley of Death
   Rode the six hundred.
'Forward the Light Brigade!
Charge for the guns!' he said.
Into the valley of Death
   Rode the six hundred.

'Forward, the Light Brigade!'
Was there a man dismay'd?
Not tho' the soldier knew
   Someone had blunder'd.
Theirs not to make reply,
Theirs not to reason why,
Theirs but to do and die.
Into the valley of Death
   Rode the six hundred.

Cannon to right of them,
Cannon to left of them,
Cannon in front of them
   Volley'd and thunder'd;
Storm'd at with shot and shell,
Boldly they rode and well,
Into the jaws of Death,
Into the mouth of hell
   Rode the six hundred.

Flash'd all their sabres bare,
Flash'd as they turn'd in air
Sab'ring the gunners there,
Charging an army, while
   All the world wonder'd.
Plunged in the battery-smoke
Right thro' the line they broke;
Cossack and Russian
Reel'd from the sabre-stroke
   Shatter'd and sunder'd.
Then they rode back, but not,
   Not the six hundred.

Cannon to right of them,
Cannon to left of them,
Cannon behind them
   Volley'd and thunder'd;
Storm'd at with shot and shell,
While horse and hero fell,
They that had fought so well
Came thro' the jaws of Death,
Back from the mouth of hell,
All that was left of them,
   Left of six hundred.

When can their glory fade?
O the wild charge they made!
   All the world wonder'd.
Honor the charge they made!
Honor the Light Brigade,
   Noble six hundred!

Robert Browning
1812 - 1889

The poems of Robert Browning expose readers to murderers, manipulative bishops and cunning painters. Happy and well educated, Browning distanced himself from these eccentric characters through the dramatic monologue format. He led a charmed life, although Henry James noted at the time of Browning's death that, "none of the odd ones have been so great and none of the great ones have been so odd."

Encouraged by genial parents who loved books and music, Browning was educated in their London suburban home, with its six thousand books. His early poems were very odd and generally ignored; as Browning commented, "cursed by the tens, and unmeddled with by the hundreds." When he wrote letters of admiration, and later passion, to Elizabeth Barrett in 1845, she was the notable poet of the two. Their courtship and elopement away from her tyrannical father has become a romantic legend for the ages, captured in the movie *The Barretts of Wimpole Street*. She lived only fifteen more years, and for her health's sake they resided in Italy. The dramatic monologues that became his forte were published in three volumes from 1845 to 1864. His masterpiece, *The Ring and the Book*, tells a murder tale in ten monologues. He was lionized in London for the remainder of his years.

Of all the Victorians, Browning most influenced modern poetry be-cause he chose unconventional subjects, did not moralize, and blurred the boundaries between prose and poetry. The language in his dramatic monologues was controlled but seemingly conversational. In "My Last Duchess" the Duke, in describing his deceased wife, reveals himself as an arrogant murderer. The speaker in "The Bishop Orders His Tomb" unwittingly informs us of his jealousies and other sins. In "Porphyria's Lover" a demented lover cheerfully tells how he strangled his girlfriend for love's sake. Browning also wrote the popular version of *The Pied Piper of Hamelin*. On more normal topics, Browning made great poetic sense, as in, "Grow old along with me!/ The best is yet to be,/ The last of life, for which the first was made:" and "a man's reach should exceed his grasp,/ Or what's a heaven for?"

The year's at the spring
And day's at the morn;
Morning's at seven;
The hill-side's dew-pearled;
The lark's on the wing;
The snail's on the thorn:
God's in his heaven –
All's right with the world!

Browning died in Venice where he was temporarily buried because the law allowed only two days until interment. He had requested burial next to his wife in Florence, but the cemetery was full. His body was transported to England, and thence to Poets' Corner and interment in front of the Chaucer sarcophagus. Browning's popularity required that tickets be shown for admission to the ceremony. Their son refused the Abbey's request to exhume the remains of Elizabeth to rest next to her husband's.

Home-Thoughts, From Abroad

Oh, to be in England
Now that April's there,
And whoever wakes in England
Sees, some morning, unaware,
That the lowest boughs and the brushwood sheaf
Round the elm-tree bole are in tiny leaf,
While the chaffinch sings on the orchard bough
In England – now!

And after April, when May follows,
And the whitethroat builds, and all the swallows!
Hark, where my blossomed pear-tree in the hedge
Leans to the field and scatters on the clover
Blossoms and dewdrops – at the bent spray's edge –
That's the wise thrush; he sings each song twice over,
Lest you should think he never could recapture
The first fine careless rapture!
And though the fields look rough with hoary dew,
All will be gay when noontide wakes anew
The buttercups, the little children's dower
– Far brighter than this gaudy melon-flower!

Thomas Hardy
1840 - 1928

Thomas Hardy, author of *The Return of the Native*, *The Mayor of Casterbridge*, *Tess of the d'Urbervilles* and *Jude the Obscure*, is often perceived as the pessimistic philosopher of determinism and the "immanent will." Hardy was also a fine poet.

Raised in Dorset, which became the Wessex of his novels, Hardy trained as an architect, tried poetry, wrote novels from 1871 to 1895, and subsequently quit novel-writing because critics hounded him over his characters' anguished relationships. In *Tess*, Angel Clare carried the dairymaids over a stream, but fastidious editors demanded a convenient wheelbarrow for the actual touching. For seduction scenes, modern readers usually need to backtrack to determine what happened, but a squeamish Victorian public howled anyway. Hardy turned to poetry for his last 33 years. He detested biographies but foresaw the inevitable, so he wrote his own and had his second wife publish it under her name after his death. She amended most of the endearing passages regarding Hardy's first wife, but it mattered little since the hoax was exposed anyway.

Hardy infused his novels with the inexorable fatalism, impersonal landscape and elevated language of a Greek tragedy. In *The Mayor of Casterbridge* Michael Henshard sells his wife and daughter, a fateful act that parallels King Lear's rash treatment of his daughters, with similar results. *Tess* exposes the double standard, when on the night of their wedding Tess and Angel Clare exchange their secrets that neither is chaste; she forgives but is not forgiven. The novel's subtitle is, "a pure woman faithfully presented." Contemporaries called Hardy's final novel "Jude the Obscene." Jude, too, is subject to the philosopher Schopenhauer's "immanent will," predestined to forsake happiness because of a foolish marriage, the penalty of which stands as a life sentence for both Jude and his lover, Sue. Hardy wrote a number of excellent poems, including "The Man He Killed" and "Hap."

Hardy's ashes were buried in Poets' Corner next to Dickens, but not before his heart was removed, stored in a biscuit tin and buried in Dorset. This gruesome compromise between Hardy's will, which named Dorset, and a clamor for the national interest was matched in crudeness only by the funeral chaos, with numerous wrong invitations and gatecrashers. Hardy's pallbearers were literary luminaries James Barrie, Rudyard Kipling, John Galsworthy, A. E. Housman, Edmund Gosse, and G. B. Shaw.

> *Yes; quaint and curious war is!*
> *You shoot a fellow down*
> *You'd treat if met where any bar is,*
> *Or help to half-a-crown.*
> *–from The Man He Killed*

From Tess of the d'Urbervilles

Feeling sideways they encountered another tower-like pillar, square and uncompromising as the first; beyond it another, and another. The place was all doors and pillars, some connected above by continuous architraves.

"A very Temple of the Winds," he said.

The next pillar was isolated, others composed a trilithon; others were prostrate, their flanks forming a causeway wide enough for a carriage; and it was soon obvious that they made up a forest of monoliths, grouped upon the grassy expanse of the plain. The couple advanced further into this pavilion of the night, till they stood in its midst.

"It is Stonehenge!" said Clare.

"The heathen temple, you mean?"

"Yes. Older than the centuries; older than the d'Urbervilles! ... Well, what shall we do, darling? We may find shelter further on."

But Tess, really tired by this time, flung herself upon an oblong slab that lay close at hand, and was sheltered from the wind by a pillar. Owing to the action of the sun during the preceding day, the stone was warm and dry, in comforting contrast to the rough and chill grass around, which had damped her skirts and shoes. "I don't want to go any further, Angel," she said stretching out her hand for his. "Can't we bide here?"

"I fear not. This spot is visible for miles by day, although it does not seem so now."

"One of my mother's people was a shepherd hereabout, now I think of it. And you used to say at Talbothays that I was a heathen. So now I am at home."

He knelt down beside her outstretched form, and put his lips upon hers. "Sleepy, are you dear? I think you are lying on an altar."

Rudyard Kipling
1865 - 1936

Rudyard Kipling was the poet of the British empire and creator of *The Jungle Book* and *Kim*. As author of "the white man's burden" and other imperialistic phrases, he is sometimes reviled even by those who quote him. In 1907 Kipling won the Nobel Prize.

Born in Bombay but educated in England, Kipling returned at age 17 to Lahore, Punjab, as a journalist. To know Kipling is to know India in its complexity and danger, where East did indeed meet West. In 1889 he left India and over the next decade lived in America, England and South Africa, where he admired strong leaders such as Teddy Roosevelt, Cecil Rhodes and Lord Milner. Kipling vigorously supported England in the Boer War and warned of the rising threat from Germany. But, Kipling's imperialism fell out of fashion. He refused the Order of Merit and the Poet Laureateship because they threatened to compromise his stand on England as the final bulwark against an encroaching barbarian world.

Kipling's stories entertain both children and adults. *The Jungle Book*, with Rikki Tikki Tavi, White Seal and Mowgli, tells didactic fairy tales. The *Just So Stories* includes "How the Rhinoceros Got His Skin." His masterpiece, *Kim*, is an adventure and a celebration of India's wonders and variety. Kipling's best adult stories, including *Barrack-Room Ballads*, portray soldiers facing danger in exotic India; "Danny Deever" is especially harrowing. "The Man Who Would Be King" may parody British imperialism. "If" and other Kipling poems blessed with strong rhythm and rhyme can become insufferable: "If you can keep your head when all about you are losing theirs ... And – which is more – you'll be a Man, my son!" "Recessional" warns against imperial pride:

God of our fathers, known of old,
Lord of our far-flung battle-line,
Beneath whose awful Hand we hold
Dominion over palm and pine–
Lord God of Hosts, be with us yet,
Lest we forget – lest we forget!

The final line became a standard military epitaph. Yet, political prejudice has largely wrecked the reputation of the poet who told us: "Oh, East is East and West is West and never the twain shall meet" and "You're a better man than I am, Gunga Din!"

The poet of the empire died two days prior to King George V, so Kipling's funeral arrangements were back-page news. His ashes were buried in Poets' Corner next to Dickens and Hardy; pallbearers included the Prime Minister and other men of action, who sang "Recessional." His original stone bore merely "R.K. 1865-1936," although it was replaced in 1965 with his full name. At the time it was common to say that "the King has gone and taken his trumpeter with him."

from Mandalay

By the old Moulmein Pagoda, lookin' lazy at the sea,
There's a Burma girl a-settin', and I know she thinks o' me;
For the wind is in the palm-trees, and the temple-bells they say:
'Come you back, you British soldier; come you back to Mandalay!'
    Come you back to Mandalay,
    Where the old Flotilla lay:
    Can't you 'ear their paddles chunkin' from Rangoon to Mandalay?
    On the road to Mandalay,
    Where the flyin'-fishes play,
    An' the dawn comes up like thunder outer China 'crost the Bay!

But that's all shove be'ind me – long ago an' fur away,
An' there ain't no 'buses runnin' from the Bank to Mandalay;
An' I'm learnin' 'ere in London what the ten-year soldier tells:
'If you've 'eard the East a-callin', you won't never 'eed naught else.'
    No! you won't 'eed nothin' else
    But them spicy garlic smells,
    An' the sunshine an' the palm-trees an' the tinkly temple-bells;
    On the road to Mandalay,
    Where the flyin'-fishes play,
    An' the dawn comes up like thunder outer China 'crost the Bay!
      . . .

Ship me somewheres east of Suez, where the best is like the worst,
Where there aren't no Ten Commandments an' a man can raise a thirst;
For the temple-bells are callin', an' it's there that I would be –
By the old Moulmein Pagoda, lookin' lazy at the sea;
    On the road to Mandalay,
    Where the old Flotilla lay,
    With our sick beneath the awnings when we went to Mandalay!
    On the road to Mandalay,
    Where the flyin'-fishes play,
    An' the dawn comes up like thunder outer China 'crost the Bay!

John Masefield
1878 - 1967

John Masefield, an old-fashioned storyteller in both verse and prose, is most famous for poems about the sea. Remarkably, he was England's first sailor-poet. Masefield was named Poet Laureate in 1930.

Because both parents died when he was young, Masefield entered the merchant marines at age 13, in the final days of the tall-masted ships. He quit the sea at 17 and published *Salt Water Ballads* in 1902, a collection that included "Sea Fever," "Trade Winds" and "A Wanderer's Song." For Masefield, "the sea creates stories." At 22 he became friends with poet William Butler Yeats and dramatist John Millington Synge. His prodigious literary output over the rest of his life included short stories, long verse narratives in ballad style, novels and plays. In World War I he served with the Red Cross at Gallipoli and wrote a history of the disaster. During World War II he celebrated Dunkirk in *The Nine Days Wonder*. Masefield saw grace in man's struggle – at sea, at war, even in defeat. Masefield was married for 57 years; their son was killed in the second world war.

With verse forms that were regular, metrical and readable and subjects that were very English, Masefield's poems were out of date and out of style even while he was writing. But, they were very popular. "Cargoes" is an exquisite short poem. His long verse narratives, *The Everlasting Mercy*, *The Widow in the Bye Street* and *Dauber*, contain rough language that disturbed some readers in 1911-13. *Dauber* depicts a young artist who goes to sea and ends tragically when he is taunted into proving his mettle. "The Wanderer" admiringly portrays a jinxed ship and its crew's lost journey. Masefield was the last major narrative English poet, very unmodern at a time when Ezra Pound and others were altering the forms and subjects of poetry. He was a balladist, not an egoist. *Reynard the Fox*, perhaps his best long narrative poem – this time about the hunt, survival, and the English countryside – includes Chaucerian vignettes as well as his allegory of the fox.

The old poet died after he refused amputation to forestall gangrene. A month after his death, Masefield's ashes were interred in Poets' Corner, next to Browning.

Sea Fever

I must go down to the seas again, to the lonely sea and the sky,
And all I ask is a tall ship and a star to steer her by,
And the wheel's kick and the wind's song and the white sail's shaking,
And a gray mist on the sea's face and a gray dawn breaking.

I must go down to the seas again, for the call of the running tide
Is a wild call and a clear call that may not be denied;
And all I ask is a windy day with the white clouds flying,
And the flung spray and the blown spume, and the seagulls crying.

I must go down to the seas again to the vagrant gypsy life,
To the gull's way and the whale's way where the wind's like a whetted knife;
And all I ask is a merry yarn from a laughing fellow-rover,
And a quiet sleep and a sweet dream when the long trick's over.

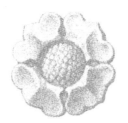

Other Poets in the Abbey

Aphra Behn
c. 1640 - 1689

Aphra Behn was the first Englishwoman to earn a living by writing. Nothing is known for certain about her early life. We think she sailed to Surinam, where her father died and she took the next ship home. Apparently she married a Mr. Behn, who died soon after, although she never mentions him by name. We know she was a spy in Holland for Charles II, sent to uncover Dutch plans against England, and she was once imprisoned for debts. Then Behn began writing for the stage, a bold act for a woman. *The Rover* and other plays were satires directed against the Whigs. She was attacked, of course: her critics called the works lascivious and her a strumpet. But, from 1676 to 1682, four or five Behn dramas played the London stage each year. Her arrest for the epilogue to *Romulus & Hersilia* ended her playwrighting career. Today Behn is read for her novel *Oroonoko*, an original story about a noble native prince and his love for Imoinda, who endure treachery on the part of English planters in Surinam and finally slavery and death.

Behn died impoverished and was buried, not in Poets' Corner, but in the Cloisters of Westminster Abbey, alongside two great actors of the day, Thomas Betterton and Anne Bracegirdle. Over two centuries later, Virginia Woolf wrote, "All women together ought to let flowers fall upon the grave of Aphra Behn."

from Oroonoko

And these people represented to me an absolute idea of the first
state of innocence, before man knew how to sin: And 'tis most
evident and plain that simple Nature is the most harmless, inoffen-
sive and vertuous mistress. 'Tis she alone, if she were permitted,
that better instructs the world than all the inventions of man.
Religion wou'd here but destroy that tranquillity they possess by
ignorance; and laws wou'd but teach 'em to know offense, of
which now they have no notion. They once made mourning and
fasting for the death of the English governor, who had given his
hand to come on such a day to 'em, and neither came nor sent,
believing when once a man's word was passed, nothing but death
cou'd or shou'd prevent his keeping it. And when they saw he was
not dead, they ask'd him what name they had for a man who
promis'd a thing he did not do. The governor told them, such a
man was a lyar, which was a word of infamy to a gentleman.
Then one of 'em reply'd, *Governor, you are a lyar, and guilty of
that infamy.*

John Gay
1685 - 1732

John Gay collaborated with Alexander Pope and Jonathan Swift to ridicule the false tastes and pedantry of rival wits and poets. Their verse satires and farcical plays were the hit of fashionable London. Gay's masterpiece, *The Beggar's Opera*, was all his own. A ballad opera – and a burlesque on Italian operas – it was the first musical comedy, preceding Gilbert and Sullivan and then Broadway by two centuries. *The Beggar's Opera* is sympathetic to low life – whores and thieves – with satirical digs at the Whig prime minister, Robert Walpole. Walpole banned the sequel, *Polly*. Bertolt Brecht and Kurt Weill's *The Three Penny Opera* is a 20th-century adaptation, from which Bobby Darin later sang "Mack the Knife."

The congenial Gay wrote "My Own Epitaph" a dozen years before his death:

> Life is a jest; and all things show it.
> I thought so once; but now I know it.

which Pope took care to see inscribed on Gay's monument. Of course the lines met with disapprobation, but they stayed in place until 1936 when two medieval wall paintings were discovered behind Gay's tablet. To regain a view of the murals, Gay's jest was transferred to the Triforium (the gallery above the aisles and ambulatory), which is off-limits to visitors for safety reasons. The exact spot of Gay's burial is unknown, but it is recorded as being on the right side of Thomas Parr, in front of Händel.

from The Beggar's Opera

MRS. PEACHUM: Captain Macheath is very fond of the girl.

PEACHUM: And what then?

MRS. PEACHUM: If I have any skill in the ways of women, I am sure Polly thinks him a very pretty man.

PEACHUM: And what then? You would not be so mad to have the wench marry him! Gamesters and highwaymen are generally very good to their whores, but they are very devils to their wives.

MRS. PEACHUM: But if Polly should be in love, how should we help her, or how can she help herself? Poor girl, I am in the utmost concern about her.

Air IV
If love the virgin's heart invade,
How, like a moth, the simple maid
Still plays about the flame!
If soon she be not made a wife,
Her honor's singed, and then for life
She's – what I dare not name.

Air IV (Why is your faithful slave disdained?)   Giovanni Battista Buononcini

Edward Bulwer-Lytton
1803-1873

Edward Bulwer-Lytton was originally just Edward Bulwer but added Lytton (his mother's name) when he was created a baronet at age 35. His marriage severed his ties with his mother, as well as with his family allowance. So, young Bulwer wrote and wrote and wrote. His early novels, such as *Pelham, Paul Clifford* and *Godolphin*, were didactic character studies. Within a decade he separated from his wife, who then caricatured him bitterly in her own novel. Bulwer served in Parliament and wrote more novels, including a suspenseful *The Last Days of Pompeii*, which captured the spirit more than the exactitude of the historical event. His study, *England and the English*, and his later novels, such as *The Caxtons*, portrayed English society. He re-entered Parliament for another fourteen years. At that time, Bulwer-Lytton was as popular as he is now forgotten. He was offered the throne of Greece, but declined.

However, Bulwer-Lytton left his mark, for it was he who convinced Dickens to change the unhappy ending to *Great Expectations*. He also coined the phrase, "The pen is mightier than the sword." But, he is most famous for the opening lines to *Paul Clifford*, "It was a dark and stormy night, the rain fell in torrents." We expect "And a shot rang out" to follow, but that is only the parody in the *Peanuts* cartoon strip – Snoopy lying supine on the doghouse roof, pondering his own melodramatic novel. In America, San Jose State University sponsors the annual Bulwer-Lytton writing contest, with hundreds of entrants submitting the *best* "awful" opening paragraph for a novel.

Edward, 1st Baron Lytton was buried in the Chapel of St. Edmund, alongside nobles from many centuries past. The Chapel is just south of the Confessor's shrine, along the South Ambulatory.

from Pelham

Vulgar people know nothing of the necessaries required in good society, and the credit they give is as short as their pedigree. Six years after my birth, there was an execution in our house. My mother was just setting off on a visit to the Duchess of D____; she declared it was impossible to go without her diamonds. The chief of the bailiffs declared it was impossible to trust them out of his sight. The matter was compromised – the bailiff went with my mother to C____, and was introduced as *my tutor*. "A man of singular merit," whispered my mother, "but *so* shy!" Fortunately the bailiff was abashed, and by losing his impudence he kept the secret. At the end of the week the diamonds went to the jeweller's, and Lady Frances wore paste.

I think it was about a month afterwards that a sixteenth cousin left my mother twenty thousand pounds. "It will just pay off our most importunate creditors, and equip me for Melton," said Mr. Pelham.

What's a Nice Girl Like You Doing in a Place Like This?

Some monuments and dedications in Poets' Corner are surprising because they present us with people we do not expect to be here. And they are not here – just their dedicatory plaques.

George Eliot
1819 - 1880

George Eliot was an atheist. She was also a genius *extraordinaire* who, along with Dickens, was the supreme novelist of the mid-Victorian period. Her real name was Mary Ann Evans. Eliot's novels include *Adam Bede, The Mill on the Floss, Silas Marner*, and *Middlemarch*. She also wrote intellectual reviews on sociology and psychology (sciences then in their infancy), among other topics. Eliot was buried at Highgate Cemetery.

from Silas Marner

He seated himself on his fireside chair, and was stooping to push his logs together, when, to his blurred vision, it seemed as if there were gold on the floor in front of the hearth. Gold! – his own gold – brought back to him as mysteriously as it had been taken away! He felt his heart begin to beat violently, and for a few moments he was unable to stretch out his hand and grasp the restored treasure. The heap of gold seemed to glow and get larger beneath his agitated gaze. He leaned forward at last, and stretched forth his hand; but instead of the hard coin with the familiar resisting outline, his fingers encountered soft warm curls. In utter amazement, Silas fell on his knees and bent his head low to examine the marvel: it was a sleeping child – a round, fair thing, with soft yellow rings all over its head.

Oscar Wilde
1854 - 1900

Wilde's dramatic wit was matched only by his own dazzling conversation. His scintillating comedies include *Lady Windermere's Fan*, *An Ideal Husband* and *The Importance of Being Earnest*. "There is no such thing as a moral or an immoral book. Books are well written, or badly written," wrote Wilde in *The Picture of Dorian Gray*, the story of a man whose portrait ages while he remains forever beautiful. Wilde was sent to prison for homosexuality and died shortly after his release. He was buried in Paris.

from The Importance of Being Earnest

LADY BRACKNELL: I have always been of opinion that a man who desires to get married should know either everything or nothing. Which do you know?

JACK: [hesitates] I know nothing, Lady Bracknell.

LADY BRACKNELL: I am pleased to hear it. I do not approve of anything that tampers with natural ignorance. Ignorance is like a delicate exotic fruit; touch it and the bloom is gone. The whole theory of modern education is radically unsound. Fortunately in England, at any rate, education produces no effect whatsoever. If it did, it would prove a serious danger to the upper classes, and probably lead to acts of violence in Grosvenor Square. What is your income?

Gerard Manley Hopkins
1844 - 1889

Hopkins was a Jesuit, serving his Order as a missionary in the slums of Liverpool and as a Greek professor at the new Catholic University College. His poems, such as "God's Grandeur" and "The Windhover," are notable for an idiosyncratic meter, which he called "sprung rhythm," where the number of stresses is set but the disposition of unstressed syllables varies. He considered this a combination of speech and song. Hopkins was buried in Dublin and his poems not published until 1918.

Pied Beauty

Glory be to God for dappled things –
   For skies of couple-colour as a brinded cow;
    For rose-moles all in stipple upon trout that swim;
Fresh-firecoal chestnut-falls, finches' wings;
   Landscape plotted and pieced – fold, fallow, and plough;
    And áll trádes, their gear and tackle and trim.

All things counter, original, spare, strange;
   Whatever is fickle, freckled (who knows how?)
    With swift, slow; sweet, sour; adazzle, dim;
He fathers-forth whose beauty is past change:
                     Praise him.

D.H. Lawrence
1885 - 1930

Lawrence decried the replacement of old agrarian England by its new industrial substitute. After World War I he roamed Europe, Australia and America as an isolated modern artist. *Sons and Lovers* was his autobiographical novel, which along with *The Rainbow, Women in Love* and *Lady Chatterley's Lover*, spoke to the deepest Freudian drives within us. He changed the face of fiction, but his novels were banned, of course. Lawrence died of tuberculosis in southern France; in 1935 his ashes were transported to New Mexico.

from Lady Chatterley's Lover

And however one might sentimentalize it, this sex business was one of the most ancient, sordid connections and subjections. Poets who glorified it were mostly men. Women had always known there was something better, something higher. And now they knew it more definitely than ever. The beautiful pure freedom of a woman was infinitely more wonderful than any sexual love. The only unfortunate thing was that men lagged so far behind women in the matter. They insisted on the sex thing like dogs.

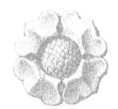

The Abbey's Wide Embrace

Lord Byron - 1969

Laurence Olivier - 1991

Elizabeth Gaskell - 2010

Ted Hughes - 2011

A poet – author, actor, artist, composer – can be honored in Poets' Corner in two ways, burial here or installation of a commemorative window, plaque or floor stone. Today both burial and commemoration in the Abbey represent affirmation of the individual's achievements and influence on British culture and acceptance as a human being, warts and all. This was not always the case when the mores of church and society required probity at least in public, a sine qua non no matter what artistic level was achieved. Libertines, divorcees, non-Anglicans, radicals and the like need not apply; drinkers were all right, of course. Today the Abbey considers the merits of the whole person.

All four of the inductees discussed here required balanced judgments to usher their way into Poets' Corner. Inclusion is the Dean's decision alone, but he consults experts. The most recent of the four, poet Ted Hughes, received fervent support from an elder statesman of poetry, Seamus Heaney, a Nobelist in literature and former Professor of Poetry at both Oxford and Harvard.

Actual burial – today only ashes are interred in the finite space left in the Abbey – is different from a memorial, which can be celebrated long after the deceased is buried elsewhere. One guideline for installing a memorial is a ten-year wait after death, but this is optional, not decreed. Two of our recent four were memorialized a century and a half after their deaths. Lord Byron, the Romantic poet, was included after cynics observed that Boatswain, his Newfoundland dog, had a far nobler monument than the poet himself. Boatswain's ashes are housed in an urn above Byron's verse paean that is lengthier and more heartfelt than people write about each other, its final lines:

Monument to Boatswain.

> Oh man! thou feeble tenant of an hour,
> Debas'd by slavery, or corrupt by power.
> Who knows thee well, must quit thee with disgust,
> Degraded mass of animated dust!
> Thy love is lust, thy friendship all a cheat,
> Thy tongue hypocrisy, thy words deceit.
> By nature vile, ennobled but by name,
> Each kindred brute might bid thee blush for shame.
> Ye! who behold perchance this simple urn,
> Pass on, it honours none you wish to mourn.
> To mark a friend's remains these stones arise.
> I never knew but one and here he lies.

Lord Byron
1788-1824

When Byron's eyes were closed in death
We bowed our heads and held our breath;
He taught us little, but our soul
Had felt him like the thunder's roll.
— Matthew Arnold (1850)

Lord Byron in
Albanian dress.

George Gordon, Lord Byron, author of *Don Juan*, died in Greece, engaged in its war for independence from Turkey. He was 36. Byron's heart was buried there where he was adored as a national hero, and his body shipped home to a different reception.

"Mad, bad, and dangerous to know" said those who endured Byron's libertine and profligate ways. Acceptance by the Church and society was impossible then, seen in the Dean's rebuff of Byron's petitioners for an Abbey burial: "Carry the body away and say as little about it as possible." Byron was laid to rest in the family vault in St. Mary Magdalene Church, Hucknall Torkard, Nottinghamshire.

Not everyone was too moral for Byron: Alfred Tennyson was 15 when the news arrived: "Byron was dead! I thought the whole world was at an end. I thought everything was over and finished for every one – that nothing else mattered. I remember I walked out alone, and carved 'Byron is dead' into the sandstone." In Nottinghamshire the funeral procession extended for a quarter of a mile and thousands turned out to pay their respects.

Byron's satires and un-English sentiments could be hard to take in spite of his noble impulses. In a speech to the House of Lords, Byron urged restraint in retaliating against Luddites, calling the sword "the worst argument that can be used" against these rioters who wrecked factory machines that robbed them of their livelihoods. He also voiced early opposition to Lord Elgin's looting of the Parthenon Marbles.

In *Childe Harold's Pilgrimage*, Byron penned his own portrait: "I have not loved the world, nor the world me; /I have not flatter'd its rank breath, nor bow'd/To its idolatries a patient knee."

In 1881 the King of Greece ordered a marble plaque inlaid with brass set into the chancel floor of St. Mary Magdalene Church, and in 2008 Greek Parliament declared April 19 – the date of Byron's death – as its annual Philhellenism and International Solidarity Day.

Petitioners for Byron were rejected again in 1924, the centennial of his death, but time moves on and in response to the Poetry Society's request in 1969, the Dean approved Byron's memorial stone in the Abbey floor.

She walks in beauty, like the night
Of cloudless climes and starry skies;
And all that's best of dark and bright
Meet in her aspect and her eyes:
Thus mellowed to that tender light
Which heaven to gaudy day denies.

Don Juan was as popular as it was long (16,000 lines), published piecemeal and unfinished at Byron's death. Readers then thought it sensuous and scandalous; today we read it for its fun rhythms and rhymes, occasional nuggets ("For truth is always strange; stranger than fiction"), neologisms (e.g., blasé), and the narrator persona, Byron of course.

from Don Juan, Canto 1

Juan she saw, and, as a pretty child,
    Caress'd him often—such a thing might be
Quite innocently done, and harmless styled,
    When she had twenty years, and thirteen he;
But I am not so sure I should have smiled
    When he was sixteen, Julia twenty-three;
These few short years make wondrous alterations,
Particularly amongst sun-burnt nations.

    • • •

This may seem strange, but yet 't is very common;
    For instance—gentlemen whose ladies take
Leave to o'erstep the written rights of woman,
    And break the—Which commandment is 't they break?
(I have forgot the number, and think no man
    Should rashly quote, for fear of a mistake;)
I say, when these same gentlemen are jealous,
They make some blunder, which their ladies tell us.

    • • •

Oh Plato! Plato! you have paved the way,
    With your confounded fantasies, to more
Immoral conduct by the fancied sway
    Your system feigns o'er the controlless core
Of human hearts, than all the long array
    Of poets and romancers:—You're a bore,
A charlatan, a coxcomb—and have been,
At best, no better than a go-between.

And Julia's voice was lost, except in sighs,
    Until too late for useful conversation;
The tears were gushing from her gentle eyes,
    I wish indeed they had not had occasion;
But who, alas! can love, and then be wise?
    Not that remorse did not oppose temptation;
A little still she strove, and much repented,
And whispering "I will ne'er consent"—consented.

Elizabeth Gaskell
1810-1865

Elizabeth Gaskell published her novel *North and South* in Charles Dickens's weekly magazine *Household Words*; like Dickens she was vitally interested in the plight of workers and poor people in the Industrial Age. She was already famous when Dickens wrote her in 1850:

> My Dear Mrs Gaskell, You may perhaps have seen an announcement in the papers, of my intention to start a new cheap weekly journal of general literature?… there is no living English writer whose aid I would desire to enlist, in preference to the author of Mary Barton (a book that profoundly affected and impressed me). I venture to ask whether you can give me any hope that you will write a short tale, or any number of tales, for the projected pages.

In the fashion of the day she was called Mrs. Gaskell; furthermore, she was a Mancunian – from Manchester, the most talked about industrial city in Europe, a place she knew well. Her earlier work *Mary Barton* reflected Manchester itself; *North and South* fictionalized the city into Milton, making it representative of England's cotton towns in the North.

Elizabeth Gaskell (1832)

Elizabeth was a Unitarian, a dissenting church member, and married William Gaskell, the minister at Cross Street Unitarian Chapel. They moved to Manchester with their four children and after publication of her first novel, *Cranford*, which immortalized Knutsford, the village of her birth, they settled in Plymouth Grove. From 1850 until her death from a heart attack at age 55, she wrote her books there while her husband tended to the poor.

As a friend of Charlotte Brontë (*Jane Eyre*), Elizabeth Gaskell became her first biographer at the request of Patrick Brontë, the father who outlived his wife and all six children.

Today Gaskell's house at 84 Plymouth Grove is a national attraction; Knutsford, Chesire, where Elizabeth Gaskell lies buried at Brook Street Chapel, is home to the Gaskell Society. Burial in Westminster Abbey was not sought: She belonged in the North among her Unitarian friends, even though Gaskell, ever open to valid religious experience, occasionally attended Anglican services with her daughters, so the dissenter distinction was not a finalizing factor.

On September 25, 2010, four days short of Gaskell's bicentenary, the Abbey installed her commemorative window, and her great-great-great granddaughter, Sarah Prince, laid a wreath beneath it. Elizabeth Gaskell was again among her peers.

North and South contrasts life in England's industrial north to the wealthier, more cultured south. Margaret Hale, transported north with her family to Milton, is shocked by its poverty and working conditions: "For several miles before they reached Milton, they saw a deep lead-coloured cloud hanging over the horizon..." Her deep sympathy comes into conflict with growing affection for John Thornton, owner of a cotton mill.

Steel line engraving by Edward Goodall of William Wyld's "A view of Manchester from Kersal Moor," commissioned by Queen Victoria in 1852.

from North and South

[Factory workers strike over imported Irish scab laborers]

As soon as they saw Mr. Thornton, they set up a yell, – to call it not human is nothing, – it was as the demoniac desire of some terrible wild beast for the food that is withheld from his ravening. Even he drew back for a moment, dismayed at the intensity of hatred he had provoked. 'Let them yell!' said he. 'In five minutes more—, I only hope my poor Irishmen are not terrified out of their wits by such a fiendlike noise. Keep up your courage for five minutes, Miss Hale.'

'Don't be afraid for me,' she said hastily. 'But what in five minutes? Can you do nothing to soothe these poor creatures? It is awful to see them.'

'The soldiers will be here directly, and that will bring them to reason.'

'To reason!' said Margaret, quickly. 'What kind of reason?'

'The only reason that does with men that make themselves into wild beasts. By heaven! they've turned to the mill-door!'

'Mr. Thornton,' said Margaret, shaking all over with her passion, 'go down this instant, if you are not a coward. Go down and face them like a man. Save these poor strangers, whom you have decoyed here. Speak to your workmen as if they were human beings. Don't let the soldiers come in and cut down poor-creatures who are driven mad. Go out and speak to them, man to man.'

He turned and looked at her while she spoke. A dark cloud came over his face; he set his teeth as he heard her words.

Daniela Denby-Ashe and Richard Armitage in BBC's *North and South* (2004).

Laurence Olivier
1907-1989

He was Hamlet. He was Heathcliff. He was Henry the Fifth. Also Max de Winter, master of Mandelay, and evil dentist Dr. Szell.

He was Laurence Olivier, one of the greatest actors of the twentieth century, notable for his Shakespeare on stage and screen. Now he lies under the same roof as Henry V, England's great warrior king laid to rest in the Abbey over five centuries before Olivier portrayed him onscreen.

Olivier won his Oscars (Actor, Director) for *Hamlet*, but *Henry V* with its sterling leadership and monumental victory at Agincourt prompted Winston Churchill to request that the film's release coincide with the D-Day invasion:

> *We few, we happy few, we band of brothers;*
> *For he to-day that sheds his blood with me*
> *Shall be my brother. Be he ne'er so vile,*
> *This day shall gentle his condition;*
> *And gentlemen in England now abed*
> *Shall think themselves accursed they were not here,*
> *And hold their manhoods cheap whiles any speaks*
> *That fought with us upon Saint Crispin's day. (IV, iii, 60-67)*

In 1962 Olivier became the first artistic director of the National Theatre of Great Britain, housed at the Old Vic and then in the new National Theatre with its main stage named in Olivier's honor. His influence in British theater was enormous, comparable to David Garrick's in the 18th century and Henry Irving's at the end of the 19th century. They too are buried in front of Shakespeare's memorial, along with actress Dame Sybil Thorndike.

Knighted in 1947 and created a life peer in 1970, he insisted on "Larry," never Sir Laurence or Lord Olivier. Olivier married three times, to actresses Jill Esmond, Vivien Leigh and Joan Plowright. Baron Olivier of Brighton died at home in Sussex at age 82; a memorial service in the Abbey was held several months later with Douglas Fairbanks, Michael Caine, Peter O'Toole and Sir Alec Guiness in its procession. His ashes were interred here in 1991.

Henry V

Rebecca

Wuthering
Heights

Marathon Man

Hamlet

Ted Hughes
1930-1998

Ted Hughes's father was a rare survivor of the tragic Gallipoli campaign in World War I. The soldier's son attended Cambridge University and became a poet, acclaimed from his first book of poetry in 1957 until his death ninety books later. His works included children's stories and translations. He was named Poet Laureate in 1984.

Nature in its innocent savagery was a recurring topic for Hughes, an ardent conservationist opposing the use of Dartmoor by the military. His son, Dr. Nicholas Hughes, became an expert in freshwater fish.

I found this jawbone at the sea's edge:
There, crabs, dogfish, broken by the breakers or tossed
To flap for half an hour and turn to a crust
Continue the beginning. The deeps are cold:
In that darkness camaraderie does not hold.

– from "Relic"

Hughes's first wife, American poet Sylvia Plath, killed herself in 1963, for which Hughes caught blame from the rising Feminist Movement. Their argument ramped up when his mistress Assia Wevill killed herself and daughter in 1969. The curse continued as son Nicholas committed suicide in 2007, deeply depressed over his father's death.

In North Tawton, Devon, Hughes worked his father's farm and wrote poetry. His funeral was held there and his ashes scattered in a remote location on Dartmoor, a memorial stone hidden partly due to the poet's private nature and also to forestall desecration.

Adversaries exist today but in decreasing numbers and tumult, as Hughes's reputation as a major poet becomes secure. Critical assessments, though, even after his death range from "Ted Hughes, Talented Murderer" to "Ted Hughes, The Poet Who Is Coming In from the Cold."

Birthday Letters, published posthumously to high praise, documented Hughes's complex relationship to Plath.

> Remember how we picked the daffodils?
> Nobody else remembers, but I remember.
> Your daughter came with her armfuls, eager and happy,
> Helping the harvest. She has forgotten.
> She cannot even remember you. And we sold them.
> It sounds like sacrilege, but we sold them.
> Were we so poor? Old Stoneman, the grocer,
> Boss-eyed, his blood-pressure purpling to beetroot
> (It was his last chance,
> He would die in the same great freeze as you),
> He persuaded us. Every Spring
> He always bought them, sevenpence a dozen,
> 'A custom of the house'.

Crossing The Bar

Sunset and evening star,
  And one clear call for me!
And may there be no moaning of the bar,
  When I put out to sea,

But such a tide as moving seems asleep,
  Too full for sound and foam,
When that which drew from out the boundless deep
  Turns again home.

Twilight and evening bell,
  And after that the dark!
And may there be no sadness of farewell,
  When I embark;

For tho' from out our bourne of Time and Place
  The flood may bear me far,
I hope to see my Pilot face to face
  When I have crost the bar.

– Alfred Lord Tennyson

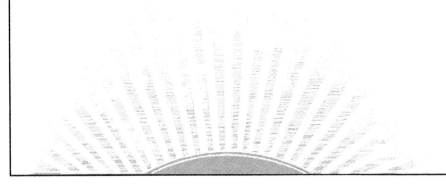

About the Author

Dr. Joel W. Athey is Professor Emeritus at California State University, Northridge, where he taught Victorian Literature and Bibliography and Research Methods. Professor Athey was born and raised in Kansas, the heartland of America.

Special thanks to Yolanda Kirk for editing and Sylvia Portillo for original artwork. Photo of the Johnson Dictionary from the Oviatt Library, California State University, Northridge.

*Tennyson's bust
in Westminster Abbey*